Ecosystems Research Journal

The Amazon Rain Forest

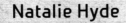

Natalie Hyde

CRABTREE
Publishing Company
www.crabtreebooks.com

Crabtree Publishing Company
www.crabtreebooks.com

Author: Natalie Hyde

Editors: Sonya Newland, Kathy Middleton

Design: Rocket Design (East Anglia) Ltd

Cover design: Margaret Amy Salter

Proofreader: Angela Kaelberer

**Production coordinator and
    prepress technician:** Margaret Amy Salter

Print coordinator: Margaret Amy Salter

Consultant:

Written and produced for Crabtree Publishing Company
by White-Thomson Publishing

Front Cover:

Title Page:

Photo Credits:

Cover: All images from Shutterstock

Interior: Alamy: p. 19 Reuters, p. 24b blickwinkel; Ron Dixon:
p. 4; iStock: p. 8bl Nastasic, p. 17b Panmaule, p. 26b Nikola
Nastasic; Shutterstock: p. 2t Salparadis, p. 2bl terekhov igor, p.
2br Dirk Ercken, p. 6 Mirek Nowaczyk, p. 7t guentermanaus, p.
7bl Frontpage, p. 8t Christian Vinces, p. 8br guentermanaus, p.
9t Christian Vinces, p. 10t Rafal Cichawa, p. 10b Hein Nouwens,
p. 11t Fiona Ayerst, p. 11b Ryan M. Bolton, p. 12t Matyas Rehak,
p. 12bl Milkovasa, p. 12br Jess Kraft, p. 13t Steve Cukrov, p.
13b Andrea Izzotti,p. 14t Scott Biales, p. 14b matyas, p. 15t
Pan Xunbin, p. 15m XEG, p. 15b JustinDutcher, p. 16t Mariusz
S. Jurgielewicz, p. 16b luckypic, p. 17r Ammit Jack, p. 18
Anton_Ivanov, pp. 18–19 Lukasz Janyst, p. 20t Ammonite, p.
20b Ivan Kuzmin, p. 21t Calek, p. 21b Grigory Kubatyan, p. 22t
Filipe Frazao, p. 22b MariaCheri, p. 23t Christian Vinces, p. 23b
Hans Wagemaker, p. 24t guentermanaus, p. 25b Ryan M. Bolton,
p. 26t Mariano Villafane, p. 27t Vadim Petrakov, p. 28tl Anton_
Ivanov, p. 28tr guentermanaus, pp. 28–29 Mykola Gomeniuk, p.
29t Ammit Jack; Wikimedia: p. 27b Feroze Omardeen.

Library and Archives Canada Cataloguing in Publication

CIP available at the Library and Archives Canada

Library of Congress Cataloging-in-Publication Data

Names: Hyde, Natalie, 1963- author.
Title: Amazon rainforest research journal / Natalie Hyde.
Description: New York, New York : Crabtree Publishing Company,
    2018. |
Series: Ecosystems research journal | Includes index.
Identifiers: LCCN 2017029302 (print) | LCCN 2017030830 (ebook) |
    ISBN 9781427119278 (Electronic HTML)
    ISBN 9780778734673 (reinforced library binding : alkaline paper)
    ISBN 9780778734925 (paperback : alkaline paper)
Subjects: LCSH: Amazon River Valley--Environmental conditions--
    Research--Juvenile literature. | Rain forests--Research--Amazon
    River Valley--Juvenile literature. | Biotic communities--Research-
    -Amazon River Valley--Juvenile literature. | Ecology--Research--
    Amazon River Valley--Juvenile literature. | Amazon River Valley--
    Description and travel--Juvenile literature.
Classification: LCC GE160.A434 (ebook) |
    LCC GE160.A434 H93 2018 (print) | DDC 577.340981/1--dc23
LC record available at https://lccn.loc.gov/2017029302

Crabtree Publishing Company

www.crabtreebooks.com   1-800-387-7650   Printed in Canada/082017/EF20170629

Published in Canada
Crabtree Publishing
616 Welland Ave.
St. Catharines, Ontario
L2M 5V6

Published in the United States
Crabtree Publishing
PMB 59051
350 Fifth Avenue, 59th Floor
New York, New York 10118

Published in the United Kingdom
Crabtree Publishing
Maritime House
Basin Road North, Hove
BN41 1WR

Published in Australia
Crabtree Publishing
3 Charles Street
Coburg North
VIC, 3058

Contents

Mission to the Amazon

I am packing for another adventure! As a **conservation ecologist**, I study how to preserve the relationship between living things and their environment. I have been asked by the Amazon Research Association to observe the effects of **deforestation** in the Amazon rain forest. Deforestation means cutting down forests or a group of trees. I will start my journey in Peru and end where the mighty Amazon River meets the Atlantic Ocean in Brazil. As I make my way down the longest river in the world, I will note any changes to different types of habitats. I have been asked to report on how deforestation is affecting:

- plants and animals
- the health of the habitat
- nesting sites
- **indigenous** people
- **climate change**.

The Association also wants me to report on any new projects that are having a positive effect on preserving this **ecosystem**.

4

I want to confirm some facts about the Amazon rain forest before I leave. It is the largest tropical rain forest in the world at over 1.4 billion acres (5.5 million square kilometers). Over half of

it is in Brazil. It also crosses the borders of eight other countries in South America. These countries include Peru, Ecuador, and Colombia.

There is a link between the health of the Amazon rain forest and the health of the planet. Earth is becoming warmer because too much of the gas carbon dioxide is building up in the planet's **atmosphere**. This is called global warming. Humans and animals breathe out carbon dioxide. Plants take in this gas. A large rain forest can take in a lot of carbon dioxide to prevent the planet from warming up. It also helps keep the average weather conditions around the world from changing quickly. The rain forest is also home to about half of the animal and plant species on Earth.

I am looking forward to seeing animals such as parrots and poison frogs in the rain forest.

Field Journal: Day 1

Bus to Nauta

I arrived in Iquitos, Peru. The bus ride from the airport took about two hours to the town of Nauta on the Amazon River. I noticed dirt roads leading off into the rain forest as we bumped along the gravel highway. They look unremarkable, but some of these roads are actually the starting point of the forest's destruction. Illegal loggers cut roads into protected forests where cutting down trees is against the law. They are looking for valuable hardwood trees to sell such as mahogany and ipe, also called Brazilian walnut. Trucks loaded with logs passed us on the highway, heading toward the Amazon River. The logs will be floated downriver to sawmills. I wonder how many of these trucks contain stolen logs?

Once logging roads are cut into the rain forest, it is easier for others to travel there, too. People are now able to make their way deeper and deeper into parts of the forest that used to be impossible to reach. Farmers or ranchers move into the forest. They need to clear the land to grow crops such as soybeans or raise livestock. I saw several places where ranchers had slashed and burned the remaining trees and shrubs. This opens up space for their cattle to graze.

The Amazon rain forest is called the "Lungs of the Earth." The trees and other plants produce 20% of our planet's oxygen through the process of photosynthesis.

I could see roads winding away into the rain forest from the bus.

Causes of deforestation in the Amazon rain forest

Commercial agriculture 3%

Logging 4%

Fires, mining, roads, and dams 3%

Farming 30%

Cattle ranches 60%

Cattle ranching is the main cause of deforestation in the Amazon.

Forest of Mirrors, Pacaya Samiria National Reserve

I left Nauta by riverboat and headed up the Amazon into the Pacaya Samiria National Reserve. This is the largest protected area in Peru. I am helping a team of scientists to count the population of pink river dolphins. Their pink color acts as camouflage against the red mud of the Amazon River. Their numbers are a good way to measure the health of the whole river system.

Pink river dolphins are also known as botos. They can grow up to 9 feet (2.7 meters) long.

Sightings

I spotted a giant river otter. Protected areas are critical to helping this endangered species survive. Its habitat is disappearing due to logging and farming.

Giant river otter

We divided ourselves into teams of two. Each team took a different area of the park. We stood in our canoe and counted the dolphins as they came to the surface for air. This was not an official count of all the dolphins, but a sample. Other scientists will use the numbers from many counting teams to estimate the total population.

We met up with other scientists back on shore. They had been counting in other areas of the Amazon River. Our teams' numbers showed that the dolphin population was holding steady in our area. The other teams found there was a clear decline in pink river dolphins in other areas. These animals are often killed and used for bait, or die caught in fishing nets. Dolphin communities are also sometimes split up by dams built across rivers.

Nature reserves like Pacaya Samiria are vital for giving plants, animals, and birds like this heron a place to thrive without threats.

The Amazon Protected Areas Program in Brazil aims to protect a larger area of the forest

Phase One (2002)

69,000 square miles (180,000 square kilometers) of new protected areas

Phase Two (2012)

add 52,000 square miles (135,000 square kilometers) more newly established areas

February 2016: Total area covered:

225,082.33 square miles (582,960.56 square kilometers)

| 50,000 | 100,000 | 150,000 | 200,000 | 250,000 |

Field Journal: Day 3

There were signs of erosion all along the riverbanks.

Meeting of the Maranon and Ucayali Rivers

The Maranon and Ucayali Rivers meet to form the **headwaters** of the Amazon. I scanned the banks with my binoculars as our riverboat sailed slowly down the Maranon. I was looking for turtles. Local people told me that the number of turtles are decreasing every year because they have fewer and fewer nesting sites. As the boat came closer to the shore, I could see part of the problem. The trees near the shoreline had been cut down. Their roots once kept the sandy banks in place. Now the riverbanks have been **eroded** by the river and have very little sand.

Sightings

Rubber trees grow along the river. They are signs of the rubber boom of the past that brought many companies to the Amazon. Now most natural rubber comes from plantations in Southeast Asia.

Rubber trees

It is illegal to sell turtle eggs, but people still do so.

Farther down the river I noticed another problem for the turtles. Sandy riverbanks were being used as beaches for camps or resorts. Other parts had docks for resort boats or fishermen built over them. The more people who move into the area, the less shoreline habitat there is for animals. Indigenous people from the Amazon such as the Kuikuru have collected and eaten turtle eggs for centuries. Now these eggs are being sold in town markets, and turtle shells are sold to tourists. The increase in the collection of turtle eggs means fewer eggs to hatch into a new generation of turtles.

natstat STATUS REPORT ST456/part B

Name: Giant South American river turtle (Podocnemis expansa)

Description:
The largest river turtle in South America. Males can reach 3 feet (1 meter) in length. These turtles use their long necks to eat plants growing on the river bottom. A female will lay 90–100 soft-shelled eggs in a hole on the same sandy beach each year. Guards know where to look to find the eggs and hatchlings to protect them.

Attach photograph here →

Threats:
Over–fishing, habitat destruction, mercury poisoning from mining, pollution from growing villages.

Status:
Endangered 1992–96, now low risk but only if steps continue to be taken to protect them.

The port of Iquitos.

Moto-taxi.

City of Iquitos

Our boat docked in the port of Iquitos. This is the largest city in the world that cannot be reached by roads. I was excited to have a chance to explore it. A tour around town in a moto-taxi showed me that the city is growing rapidly. Unfortunately, it is **encroaching** on the rain forest. Trees are being cut down to make room for houses, roads, and businesses. Air and water pollution from cars, buses, and industry are affecting the wildlife in the surrounding forest. Traffic on the river has also increased. The noise and pollution from boats is endangering manatees and their habitat.

The busy city.

I visited the Manatee Rescue Center in the afternoon. Scientists and local people created the center to protect and care for all kinds of rain forest animals. Many have lost their habitat to deforestation. The parents of some young animals have been killed because of **poaching** for their meat and hides. Rescuers try to bring the animals back to health. The people who work at the center help prepare them for life back in the wild. Most are released into nature reserves, where they have some protection.

The Manatee Rescue Center educates the public about the threats that manatees face.

STATUS REPORT ST456/part B

Name: Amazonian manatee
(Trichechus inunguis)

Description:

Manatees are herbivores that grow to 10–11.5 feet (3–3.5 meters) long. They have front flippers to help them swim. They also use these to push food into their mouths and even to hug each other. Pregnancy lasts about a year, and they usually have one calf. The animal most closely related to the manatee is the elephant.

Attach photograph here ➡

Threats:
Hunted for meat and oil, loss of habitat.

Status:
Vulnerable.

Canopy walk, downriver from Iquitos

I am heading out on a canopy walk today. The canopy of the rain forest is the upper branches of the trees. Rope bridges 115 feet (35 meters) in the air run from tree to tree. I am able to observe wildlife and plants from the platforms built at each tree. The canopy layer is thick with leaves and vines, making it difficult to see. By listening closely, though, I am able to identify several species of insects, birds, and mammals by their calls, including cicadas, katydids, screaming phia, bellbirds, and howler monkeys.

Sightings

I saw a pair of harpy eagles with a nest high in a kapok tree in an area of **old-growth rain forest.** No harpy eagles seen farther downriver near the clear-cut area.

Harpy eagle

I got a good view of the rain forest canopy from the highest platform. I could see bromeliads, orchids, and several other examples of "air plants." These plants grow on trees or other plants instead of in soil. The orchids are blooming, which tells me that they are about ten years old. This means these trees have been here for a long time. I notice a large hole in the canopy toward the east. The forest had been clear-cut there and is slowly regrowing. The forest is not mature enough yet for animals that live in the canopy, such as monkeys, sloths, or iguanas, to return.

Cicadas and katydids are particularly noisy insects!

natstat STATUS REPORT
ST456/part B

Name: Epiphytes (air plants)

Threats:
Loss of habitat through deforestation.

Description:
These are plants that grow on or are attached to a living plant. Like all plants, they use photosynthesis to create energy. They gather water and nutrients from the air, instead of through roots. There are about 15,000 types of epiphytes in the rain forest. Studies have shown that the number of different epiphytes in an area increases as the forest ages. Regrowth from clear-cutting does not have many species of air plants.

Status:
Least concern.

Attach photograph here ▶

Field Journal: Day 6

Lagoon near Chichita

This morning I paddled a canoe from the boat up a side stream to a quiet **lagoon**. I wanted to document how deforestation affects fish in the Amazon. Guarumo, palm, and paucar trees grow along the banks of the lagoon. I saw little sardinhão fish near the shore jumping above the water to feed. They were eating ants that dropped from nests hanging from the trees. I paddled farther looking for more hanging nests of termites, wasps, and bees. Fewer trees along the riverbanks means less food for fish that eat insects.

We saw ant nests like this one hanging from the trees.

Part of the lagoon was marked off for a fish farm to raise fish to sell to food markets. **Enclosures** made of nets are placed in the water to contain the fish. I have noticed more and more fish farms being set up in quiet side streams, bays, and lagoons. A fish farmer was checking his fish stocks. I asked him what species of fish he was raising. He said it was tambaqui. This fish is native to the Amazon River. Wild tambaqui eat fruit that falls from rain forest trees. Deforestation has caused the number of wild tambaqui to decrease.

Fish farming is also called **aquaculture**. It helps limit deforestation because fish farms do not require land to be cleared.

Tambaqui are ideal for aquaculture because they are resistant to diseases.

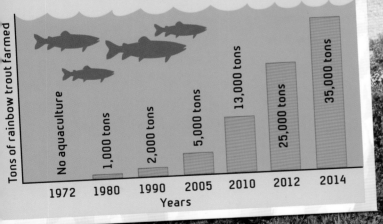

Growth of aquaculture in the Amazon basin

Tons of rainbow trout farmed

No aquaculture	1,000 tons	2,000 tons	5,000 tons	13,000 tons	25,000 tons	35,000 tons
1972	1980	1990	2005	2010	2012	2014

Years

Yavari River to Matses village

I was invited to visit a village of the Matses tribe. They are an indigenous people who live deep in the rain forest. The villagers showed me around their gardens and longhouses, called malokas. I was offered a cup of chapo, which is a drink made of the type of banana called sweet plantain. The gardens of plantains and **manioc** were cut out of the forest. The Matses hunt mammals such as tapirs and pacas for meat using bows and arrows. Medicine for everything from injury to disease is created by the villagers from the plants and animals in the rain forest.

Houses in villages are often built on stilts to keep them above the water level.

The villagers I met.

My guide spoke to the villagers. They told us about some of the threats to indigenous tribes in the Amazon rain forest. Almost all the problems are about the land. Outsiders want their land for logging or for what is underneath it: oil, gas, and minerals. They want to cut down the trees that feed, shelter, and protect the animals the villagers hunt for food. Even when governments give the tribes legal ownership of their native lands, companies and illegal loggers still take what they want without permission.

Name: Uncontacted peoples of the Amazon rain forest

Description:

Tribes that live without contact with people from the outside world. It is estimated that there are around 100 uncontacted tribes in the Amazon. They live an independent lifestyle, finding everything they need in the ecosystem around them. Sometimes, illegal loggers and miners try to take their land by force. This has led many tribes to show an unfriendly attitude toward anyone who tries to make contact with them.

The Mashco-Piru people are one of around 100 tribes classified as uncontacted.

Threats:
Habitat loss through mining and deforestation, diseases after contact with outsiders.

Status:
Vulnerable, although they thrive when their habitat is protected.

Field Journal: Day 8

Night safari in Mamiraua Nature Reserve

I arranged to go on a group expedition at night. This is a good way to observe which **nocturnal** animals rely on trees to survive. The Mamiraua Nature Reserve is a **wetland** that is part of a long strip of protected land called the Central Amazon Ecological Corridor. Many animals here spend their whole lives in the trees because the forest floor is flooded much of the year. I spied a two-toed sloth from my canoe. These sloths feed, sleep, and even have their young among the branches of the forest canopy.

As we paddled quietly, I saw the dark shadow of a bat fly overhead. Vampire bats such as the hairy-legged vampire bat roost in hollow trees and often feed on birds. I also saw a short-tailed, leaf-nosed bat. These bats eat only fruit, and seeds in their **guano** help spread tree species to new areas.

As we turned our canoes to head back, I saw something that made me catch my breath. Two yellow eyes shone in the light of my headlamp from the surface of the water. It was a black caiman. These relatives of alligators like to live in the flooded tree **mangroves**, where they can hide and there are plenty of fish to eat.

Caimans are no longer endangered thanks to laws against hunting them for their skin.

natstat STATUS REPORT ST456/part B

Name: Two-toed sloth

Description:

The slowest mammal in the world. Sloths sleep 15–20 hours a day in the branches of trees and come out at night to feed. They spend their days hanging upside down from the trees. Females even give birth that way. Young sloths cling to their mothers for several weeks. Sloths are slow-moving on land but are very good swimmers.

Threats:
Habitat loss due to deforestation.

Status:
Least concern.

Attach photograph here →

Field Journal: Day 9

Walking trail near Manaus

I was asked to join a team at a research station near Manaus to work with the Brazilian Institute for Wetland Research. I headed out today to help them gather information for a study on the importance of wetlands. First we hiked through the area to identify different types of wetlands. Some, such as marshes, have stable water levels. Other wetlands have water levels that can rise and drop up to 33 feet (10 meters) or more. For example, floodplain forests grow where rivers overflow their banks for part of the year. The water helps spread rich **sediment**.

Different wetland ecosystems support different types of grasses, trees, and animals.

Sightings

Glass frogs are a **bioindicator** species. This means healthy glass frogs are a sign that the ecosystem is also healthy. They need moisture to survive. If glass frogs are struggling, then their wetland ecosystem is becoming too dry.

Glass frog

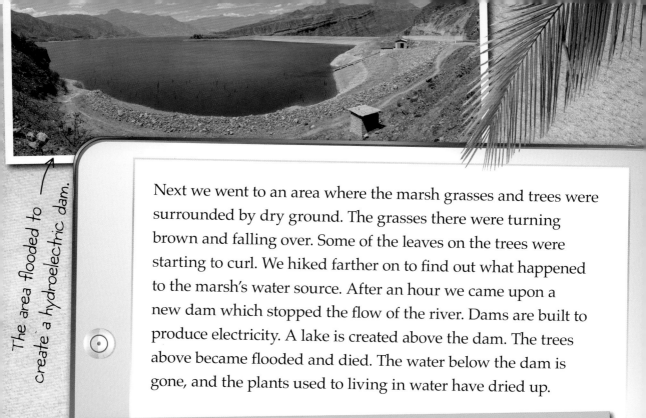

The area flooded to create a hydroelectric dam.

Next we went to an area where the marsh grasses and trees were surrounded by dry ground. The grasses there were turning brown and falling over. Some of the leaves on the trees were starting to curl. We hiked farther on to find out what happened to the marsh's water source. After an hour we came upon a new dam which stopped the flow of the river. Dams are built to produce electricity. A lake is created above the dam. The trees above became flooded and died. The water below the dam is gone, and the plants used to living in water have dried up.

natstat STATUS REPORT ST456/part B

Name: Jaguar (Panthera onca)

Description:

The largest cat in the Americas. This spotted cat prefers wetlands and deep forests. It is called a keystone species. Keystone animals are important because they control the population of the animals they hunt. Jaguars are strong swimmers, and their diet includes turtles and fish. They also hunt caimans, monkeys, tapirs, and smaller prey such as frogs, mice, and birds. They rarely attack humans, but attacks are rising as more people invade the jaguars' territory.

Threats:
Loss of habitat through deforestation, hunted as pests by ranchers and farmers.

Status:
Near threatened.

Attach photograph here ➡

The meeting of the black and white waters.

Meeting of the rivers: Rio Negro, Rio Solimões

It was amazing to see where the dark water of the Rio Negro and the white-colored water of the Rio Solimões meet. The colors stay separate and do not mix for 3.7 miles (6 kilometers). However, I am not sailing that far. I am going on a hike to look for the **critically endangered** Spix's macaw. Some believe that this bird is extinct in the wild. I read that one was spotted in the summer of 2016. It roosts, feeds, and nests in the Caribbean trumpet tree. If I can find the tree, I might find the bird!

Traveling deeper into the rain forest, I saw a clearing ahead. An entire section of rain forest had been clear-cut by illegal miners looking for gold. I hid in the trees. These groups can be unpredictable and violent. There were no Spix's macaws to be seen in this clear-cut forest. In fact there were no birds at all. On my hike back I saw dead fish in the stream. They had died from mercury poisoning from the mining process. I will call the Brazilian authorities when I get to Manaus. They will arrest the miners if they can find them and destroy their equipment.

Land used for legal and illegal gold mining in the Peruvian Amazon

1999	Less than 38 square miles (100 square kilometers)
2008	108 square miles (280 square kilometers)
2012	More than 195 square miles (500 square kilometers)
2016	580 square miles (1,500 square kilometers)

Sometimes local people take part in the illegal mining in the Amazon.

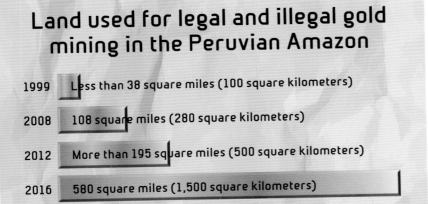

Field Journal: Day 11

The many sand spits and islands make it difficult for ships to navigate this part of the river safely.

Sail to the Amazon delta near Belem, Brazil

I have finally made it to the mouth of the Amazon River! The mouth is where the river meets the Atlantic Ocean. This area looks very different from the rain forest. There are few trees along the riverbanks. They have been cut down to make pastures for cattle. This makes the riverbanks erode more quickly. All the sediment that has been washed downriver collects at the mouth. The sand forms islands, strips of land called spits, and ridges called sandbars.

Sightings

The vegetarian piranha is an example of a recently discovered species. Scientists believe there are many more animal and plant species still to be discovered in remote parts of the Amazon.

Vegetarian piranha

Increased sediment affects the life cycles of many animals, too. Sediment may smother the water plants on which fish or manatees feed. Animals that hunt in the river for fish have difficulty finding their prey. The loss of shoreline means less habitat for **capybaras**. Farmers may cut down Amazon trees and plant non-native kinds that they can harvest for income. This leads to a loss of food for **native** animals such as deer, tapir, and fruit-eating fish.

Capybaras.

natstat STATUS REPORT ST456/part B

Name: Baboonwood tree
(Virola surinamensis)

Threats:
Habitat loss.

Description:
The leaves of the baboonwood tree are long and narrow. The fruit is a small orange ball with red flesh inside. The tree is harvested for its wood. The bark, leaves, and oil from the seeds are also valuable to local tribes as treatments for intestinal worms and malaria.

Status:
Endangered.

Attach photograph here ➡

Final Report

Report to: AMAZON RESEARCH ASSOCIATION

OBSERVATIONS

It is clear from my findings that deforestation continues to be a problem in the Amazon rain forest. Towns are growing larger, more resorts are being built, and logging and mining are increasing. Each human activity means more of the rain forest is lost.

CONSERVATION PROJECTS

Some projects and conservation measures are making a difference. Fish farming is a growing industry that requires much less land than regular farming. The use of hydroelectricity instead of burning fossil fuels has reduced pollution. National reserves have been expanded to protect half of the rain forest. More police patrols and a special satellite are helping to stop illegal activities.

Satellites are tracking the destruction of the forest.

Future Concerns

Even good ideas sometimes have drawbacks. Fish farms can disrupt the natural fish populations in an area. Hydroelectric dams can separate dolphin communities and jaguar territory. Even **ecotourism**, whose goal is to make people aware of this threatened ecosystem, brings more and more people into this sensitive area.

The rate of deforestation is slowing down, though. I hope that the plans and programs governments and people have put in place continue to make a difference.

Tourism can bring much-needed money to the area. Visitors can be encouraged to help.

Hydroelectricity plant.

The rate of deforestation is still a problem. It is slowing down thanks to laws put in place by governments.

Loss in square miles

1988   1991   1994   1997   2000   2003   2006   2009   2012   2015

Your Turn

* Journal writing tells events from one person's point of view. Pick one day's events and write them from your point of view. What things might you have noticed differently? Would you feel differently?

* Think about the importance of clean energy and the importance of not disturbing natural habitats. Write a journal entry from the point of view of someone living in a rainforest town who will soon have electricity. How might it change their life? Now write another journal entry from a member of an indigenous tribe or from the point of view of an animal whose ecosystem will be forever changed by the building of the dam.

* Take another look at one of the graphs or charts. Think about the information shown in the data. Try to write a personal encounter that could show the same idea using facts and figures. Which do you think would be more effective to get a reader to take action? Why?

Learning More

BOOKS

DK Eyewitness Books: The Amazon (DK Children, 2015).

Nature Unfolds: The Tropical Rainforest by Gerard Cheshire (Crabtree, 2001).

What's Up in the Amazon Rainforest by Ginjer L. Clarke (Grosset & Dunlap, 2015).

WEBSITES

https://www.youtube.com/watch?v=JEsV5rqbVNQ
Go on a virtual tour of the Amazon rain forest.

http://www.rainforest-alliance.org/kids
Have fun learning about the rain forest with games and activities from the Rainforest Alliance.

http://kids.mongabay.com
Learn all about why rain forests are important and how to save them with Kids at Mongabay.

Glossary & Index

aquaculture raising marine animals for food

atmosphere the layer of gases surrounding Earth

bioindicator an organism whose health is a symbol of the health of an ecosystem

capybara a South American mammal that looks like a large guinea pig

climate change a change in global climate patterns caused by increased greenhouse gases, such as carbon dioxide, in Earth's atmosphere

conservation ecologist a scientist that studies the relationship between animals, plants, and the environment

critically endangered at very high risk of extinction in the wild

deforestation clearing a large area of trees

ecosystem a community of plants, animals, and their environment

ecotourism tourism designed to protect the environment

enclosures areas sealed off with barriers

encroaching slowly moving into another area

eroded worn away

guano bat or bird droppings

headwaters the area where streams combine to form a river

indigenous native to an area

lagoon an area of salt water separated from the sea

mangroves trees that live in salt-water swamps along a shoreline

manioc the edible root of a tropical tree

native referring to something that is born in a particular place

nocturnal active at night

old-growth rainforest very old forest that has not been logged

photosynthesis the process in which plants turn sunlight into energy

poaching illegally hunting and killing

sediment a muddy substance that sinks and collects at the bottom of rivers

wetland land made up of marshes and swamps